WHAT'S THE DIFFERENCE?

VP		17	16	15	14	13	12	11	10	09	08
13	12	11	10	9	8	7	6	5	4	3	2

what's the
difference?

Manhood and Womanhood Defined According to the Bible

Foreword by Elisabeth Elliot

JOHN PIPER

CROSSWAY BOOKS

WHEATON, ILLINOIS

To Noël
my partner
in the great mystery

Contents

Foreword

For years I have noted with growing disquiet the pollution of many Christians' minds by the doctrine of feminism. I believe it is a far more dangerous pollution than most have realized, and I (with what seemed to me pitifully few others) have tried to sound the alarm in every way I could. It is a relief to me that John Piper has done what was badly needed—clarified the fundamental distinctions, defining them not fashionably but Biblically and with good common sense. He has done more— he has cut through much of the confusion that arises through a careless reading of the "difficult" Bible passages, and shown us the true liberation that comes with humble submission to God's original design. I think his thesis rings true to the manliness or the womanliness in each of us.

—*Elisabeth Elliot*

1

What's the Difference?

When I was a boy growing up in Greenville, South Carolina, my father was away from home about two-thirds of every year. And while he preached across the country, we prayed—my mother and my older sister and I. What I learned in those days was that my mother was omni-competent.

She handled the finances, paying all the bills and dealing with the bank and creditors. She once ran a little laundry business on the side. She was active on the park board, served as the superintendent of the intermediate department of our Southern Baptist church, and managed some real estate holdings.

She taught me how to cut the grass and splice electric cord and pull Bermuda grass by the roots and paint the eaves and shine the dining-room table with a shammy and drive a car and keep French fries from getting soggy in the cooking oil. She helped me with the maps in geography and showed me how to do a bibliography and work up a science project on static electricity and believe that Algebra II was possible. She dealt with the contractors when we added a basement and, more than once, put her hand to the shovel. It never occurred to me that there was anything she couldn't do.

I heard one time that women don't sweat, they glow. Not true. My mother sweated. It would drip off the end of her long, sharp nose. Sometimes she would blow it off when her hands were pushing the wheelbarrow full of peat moss. Or she would wipe it with her sleeve between the strokes of a swingblade. Mother was strong. I can remember her arms even today thirty years later. They were big, and in the summertime they were bronze.

But it never occurred to me to think of my mother and my father in the same category. Both were strong. Both were bright. Both were kind. Both would kiss me and both would spank me. Both were good with words. Both prayed with fervor and loved the Bible. But unmistakably my father was a man and my mother was a woman. They knew it and I knew it. And it was not mainly a biological fact. It was mainly a matter of personhood and relational dynamics.

When my father came home he was clearly the head of the house. He led in prayer at the table. He called the family together for devotions. He got us to Sunday School and worship. He drove the car. He guided the family to where we would sit. He made the decision to go to Howard Johnson's for lunch. He led us to the table. He called for the waitress. He paid the check. He was the one we knew we would reckon with if we broke a family rule or were disrespectful to Mother. These were the happiest times for Mother. Oh, how she rejoiced to have Daddy home! She loved his leadership. Later I learned that the Bible calls this "submission."

But since my father was gone most of the time, Mother used to do most of those leadership things too. So it never occurred to me that leadership and submission had anything to do with superiority and inferiority. And it didn't have to do with muscles and skills either. It was not a matter of capabilities and competencies. It had to do with something I could never have explained as a child. And I have been a long time in coming to understand it as part of God's great goodness in creating us male and female. It had to do with something very deep. I know that the specific rhythm of life that was in our home is not the only good one. But there were dimensions of reality and goodness in it that ought to be there in every home. Indeed they ought to be there in varying ways in all mature relationships between men and women.

I say "ought to be there" because I now see that they were rooted in God. Over the years I have come to see from Scripture and from life that manhood and womanhood are the beautiful handiwork of a good and loving God. He designed our differences and they are profound. They are not mere physiological prerequisites for sexual union. They go to the root of our personhood. This essay is an attempt to define some of those differences as God wills them to be according to the Bible.

* * * * *

Let me say a word about that phrase, "according to the Bible." The subtitle of this little book is "Manhood and Womanhood Defined *According to the Bible.*" What that means is that I have made every effort to bring the thinking of this book into accord with what the Bible teaches. At the same time, however, I have not tried to include a detailed exegetical argument for every assertion.

There are two main reasons that seem to justify this approach:

First, for the purposes of this little book, it seemed best to present the Biblical vision of manhood and womanhood as clearly and concisely as possible, and to leave the comprehensive technical discussion for other publications. Thus this little book was originally written as a chapter in a larger collection of essays, *Recovering Biblical Manhood and Womanhood* (published in 1990 by Crossway Books; edited by Wayne Grudem and John Piper), and this longer work provides detailed exegetical support for the vision of this smaller work.

I have also tried in articles,[1] sermons,[2] and unpublished papers to give a credible account of the Biblical foundations of what I say here.

Second, I have tried to include enough Biblical argumentation in this essay, especially in the footnotes, to show why I believe this vision of manhood and womanhood is in fact *"according to the Bible."* I hope it will be obvious that my reflections are not the creation of an independent mind, but the fruit of a tree planted firmly in the soil of constant meditation on the Word of God.

Third, experience has taught me that there are two ways to commend a vision of manhood and womanhood. One way has to do with rational argumentation concerning factual evidences. For example, an evangelical Christian wants to know, Does the Bible really teach this vision of manhood and womanhood? So one way of commending the vision is by patient, detailed, careful exegetical argumentation.

But there is another way to commend the vision. A person also wants to know, Is the vision beautiful and satisfying and fulfilling? Can I live with it? This is not a bad question. Commending Biblical truth involves more than saying, "Do it because the Bible says so." That sort of commendation may result in a kind of obedience that is so begrudging and so empty of delight and hearty affirmation that the Lord is not pleased with it at all.

So there is a second task needed in winning people over

to a vision of manhood and womanhood. Not only must there be thorough exegesis, there must also be a portrayal of the vision that satisfies the heart as well as the head. Or to put it another way: we must commend the beauty as well as the truth of the vision. We must show that something is not only right but also good. It is not only valid but also valuable, not only accurate but also admirable.

This little book is meant to fit *mainly* into the second category. Not merely, but mainly. It is designed to show that our vision of manhood and womanhood is a deeply satisfying gift of grace from a loving God who has the best interests of his creatures at heart. The vision is not onerous or oppressive. It does not promote pride or self-exaltation. It conforms to who we are by God's good design. Therefore it is fulfilling in the deepest sense of that word.

* * * * *

The tendency today is to stress the equality of men and women by minimizing the unique significance of our maleness or femaleness. But this depreciation of male and female personhood is a great loss. It is taking a tremendous toll on generations of young men and women who do not know what it means to be a man or a woman. Confusion over the meaning of sexual personhood today is epidemic. The consequence of this confusion is not a free and happy harmony among gender-free persons relating on the basis of abstract competencies. The consequence rather is more divorce, more homosexuality, more sexual abuse, more promiscuity, more social awkwardness, and more emotional distress and suicide that come with the loss of God-given identity.

It is a remarkable and telling observation that contemporary Christian feminists devote little attention to the definition of femininity and masculinity. Little help is being given to a son's question, "Dad, what does it mean to be a man and not a woman?" Or a daughter's question, "Mom, what does it mean to be woman and not a man?" A lot of energy is being expended today minimizing the distinctions of manhood and womanhood. But we do not hear very often what manhood and womanhood *should* incline us to do. We are adrift in a sea of confusion over sexual roles. And life is not the better for it.

Ironically the most perceptive thinkers recognize how essential manhood and womanhood are to our personhood. Yet the meaning of manhood and womanhood is seen as unattainable. For example, Paul Jewett, in his very insightful book, *Man as Male and Female,* argues persuasively that maleness and femaleness are essential, not peripheral, to our personhood:

> Sexuality permeates one's individual being to its very depth; it conditions every facet of one's life as a person. As the self is always aware of itself as an 'I,' so this 'I' is always aware of itself as *himself* or *herself.* Our self-

knowledge is indissolubly bound up not simply with our *human* being but with our *sexual* being. At the human level there is no 'I and thou' *per se*, but only the 'I' who is male or female confronting the 'thou,' the 'other,' who is also male or female.[3]

He cites Emil Brunner to the same effect: "Our sexuality penetrates to the deepest metaphysical ground of our personality. As a result, the physical differences between the man and the woman are a parable of psychical and spiritual differences of a more ultimate nature."[4]

After reading these amazing statements concerning how essential manhood and womanhood are to our personhood and how sexuality "conditions every facet of one's life," it is stunning to read that Jewett does not know what manhood and womanhood are. He says,

> Some, at least, among contemporary theologians are not so sure that they know what it means to be a man in distinction to a woman or a woman in distinction to a man. It is because the writer shares this uncertainty that he has skirted the question of ontology in this study.[5]
>
> All human activity reflects a qualitative distinction which is sexual in nature. But in my opinion, such an observation offers no clue to the ultimate meaning of that distinction. It may be that we shall never know what that distinction ultimately means. But this much, at least, seems clear: we will understand the difference— what it means to be created as man or woman— only as we learn to live as man and woman in a true partnership of life.[6]

Surely this is a great sadness. We know that "sexuality permeates one's individual being to its very depth." We know that "it conditions every facet of one's life as a person." We know that every I-Thou encounter is an encounter not of abstract persons but of male or female persons. We know that physical differences are but a parable of male and female personhood. But, alas, we do not know who we are as male and female. We are ignorant of this all-pervasive dimension of our identity.

But what about Jewett's prescription for hope in the face of this stunning ignorance of who we are? He suggests that we discover who we are "as man or woman" by experiencing a "true partnership" as man *and* woman. The problem with this is that we cannot know what a "true partnership" is until we know the nature of the partners. A true partnership must be true to who the partners are. A true partnership must take into account the sexual reality "that conditions every facet of their life." We simply cannot know what a "true" partnership is until we know what truly "permeates [our] personhood to the very depths." If we are really ignorant of what true manhood and womanhood are, we have no warrant to prescribe the nature of what *true* partnership will look like.

The sexual turmoil of our culture is not surprising when we discover that our best Christian thinkers claim not to know what masculinity and femininity are, and yet acknowledge that these are among the most profound aspects of personhood that "condition every facet of one's life"! How shall parents rear daughters to be women and sons to be men when even the leading teachers of the church do not know what manhood and womanhood are?

The conviction behind this essay is that the Bible does not leave us in ignorance about the meaning of masculine and feminine personhood. God has not placed in us an all-pervasive and all-conditioning dimension of personhood and then hidden the meaning of our identity from us. He has shown us in Scripture the beauty of manhood and womanhood in complementary harmony. He has shown us the distortions and even horrors that sin has made of fallen manhood and womanhood. And he has shown us the way of redemption and healing through Christ.

To be sure, we see "through a glass dimly." Our knowledge is not perfect. We must be ever open to new light. But we are not so adrift as to have nothing to say to our generation about the meaning of manhood and womanhood and its implications for our relationships. Our understanding is that the Bible reveals the nature of masculinity and femininity by describing diverse responsibilities for man and woman while rooting these differing responsibilities in creation, not convention.

When the Bible teaches that men and women fulfil different roles in relation to each other, charging man with a unique leadership role, it bases this differentiation not on temporary cultural norms but on permanent facts of creation. This is seen less tranquillity and holiness and prayer.

spiritual advancement; that you cultivate tenderness and strength, a pattern of initiative and a listening ear; and that you accept the *responsibility* of provision and protection in the family, however you and your wife share the labor.

10. That, if you have children, you accept responsibility with your husband (or alone if necessary) to raise up children in the discipline and instruction of the Lord—children who hope in the triumph of God—sharing with your husband the teaching and discipline they need, and giving them the special attachment they crave from you, as well as that special nurturing touch and care that you alone are fitted to give.

10. That, if you have children, you accept primary responsibility, in partnership with your wife (or as a single parent), to raise up children in the discipline and instruction of the Lord—children who hope in the triumph of God; that you establish a pattern of teaching and discipline that is not solely dependent on the church or school to impart Bible knowledge and spiritual values to the children; and that you give your children the time and attention and affection

that communicates the true nature of our Father in Heaven.

11. That you not assume that secular employment is a greater challenge or a better use of your life than the countless opportunities of service and witness in the home, the neighborhood, the community, the church, and the world; that you not only pose the question: career or full-time homemaker?, but that you ask just as seriously: full-time career or freedom for ministry? That you ask: Which would be greater for the Kingdom—to work for someone who tells you what to do to make his or her business prosper, or to be God's free agent dreaming your own dream about how your time and your home and your creativity could make God's

11. That you not assume advancement and peer approval in your gainful employment are the highest values in life; but that you ponder the eternal significance of faithful fatherhood and time spent with your wife; that you repeatedly consider the new possibilities at each stage of your life for maximizing your energies for the glory of God in ministry; that you pose the question often: Is our family molded by the culture, or do we embody the values of the Kingdom of God? That you lead the family in making choices not on the basis of secular trends or upward lifestyle expectations, but on the basis of what will

business prosper? And that in all this you make your choices not on the basis of secular trends or upward lifestyle expectations, but on the basis of what will strengthen the faith of the family and advance the cause of Christ.

strengthen the faith of the family and advance the cause of Christ.

12. That you step back and (with your husband, if you are married) plan the various forms of your life's ministry in chapters. Chapters are divided by various things—age, strength, singleness, marriage, employment, children at home, children in college, grandchildren, retirement, etc. No chapter has all the joys. Finite life is a series of trade-offs. Finding God's will, and living for the glory of Christ to the full in every chapter is what makes it a success, not whether it reads

12. That you step back and (with your wife, if you are married) plan the various forms of your life's ministry in chapters. Chapters are divided by various things—age, strength, singleness, marriage, employment, children at home, children in college, grandchildren, retirement, etc. No chapter has all the joys. Finite life is a series of trade-offs. Finding God's will and living for the glory of Christ to the full in every chapter is what makes it a success, not whether it reads

like somebody else's chapter
or whether it has in it what
only another chapter will
bring.

13. That you develop a
wartime mentality and lifestyle; that you never forget
that life is short, that billions
of people hang in the balance
of Heaven and Hell every day,
that the love of money is spiritual suicide, that the goals of
upward mobility (nicer
clothes, cars, houses, vaca-
tions, food, hobbies) are a
poor and dangerous substi-
tute for the goals of living for
Christ with all your might
and maximizing your joy in
ministry to people's needs.

14. That in all your relationships with men (not just in
marriage) you seek the guidance of the Holy Spirit in
applying the Biblical vision of
manhood and womanhood;

like somebody else's chapter
or whether it has in it what
only another chapter will
bring.

13. That you develop a
wartime mentality and lifestyle; that you never forget
that life is short, that billions
of people hang in the balance
of Heaven and Hell every day,
that the love of money is spiritual suicide, that the goals of
upward mobility (nicer
clothes, cars, houses, vaca-
tions, food, hobbies) are a
poor and dangerous substi-
tute for the goals of living for
Christ with all your might
and maximizing your joy in
ministry to people's needs.

14. That in all your relationships with women (not just
in marriage) you seek the
guidance of the Holy Spirit in
applying the Biblical vision of
manhood and womanhood;

that you develop a style and demeanor that does justice to the unique role God has given to man to feel responsible for gracious leadership in relation to women—a leadership which involves elements of protection and provision and a pattern of initiative. That you think creatively and with cultural sensitivity (just as he must do) in shaping the style and setting the tone of your interaction with men.

that you develop a style and demeanor that expresses your God-given responsibility for humble strength and leadership, and for self-sacrificing provision and protection; that you think creatively and with cultural sensitivity (just as she must do) in shaping the style and setting the tone of your interaction with women.

15. That you see the Biblical guidelines for what is appropriate and inappropriate for men and women not as arbitrary constraints on freedom, but as wise and gracious prescriptions for how to discover the true freedom of God's ideal of complementarity. That you not measure your potential by the few roles withheld, but by the count-

15. That you see the Biblical guidelines for what is appropriate and inappropriate for men and women not as license for domination or bossy passivity, but as a call to servant-leadership that thinks in terms of responsibilities not rights; that you see these principles as wise and gracious prescriptions for how to discover the true freedom of

less roles offered. That you
look to the loving God of
Scripture and dream about
the possibilities of your service to him, with the follow-
ing list as possibilities for
starters:

God's ideal of complementarity; that you encourage
the fruitful engagement of
women in the countless
ministry roles that are
Biblically appropriate and
deeply needed. For example:

OPPORTUNITIES FOR MINISTRY

Ministries to the handicapped
  Hearing impaired
  Blind
  Lame
  Retarded

Ministries to the sick
  Nursing
  Physician
  Hospice care—cancer, AIDS, etc.
  Community health

Ministries to the socially estranged
  Emotionally impaired
  Recovering alcoholics
  Recovering drug-users
  Escaping prostitutes
  Abused children, women
  Runaways, problem children
  Orphans

Prison ministries
  Women's prisons
  Families of prisoners
  Rehabilitation to society

Audiovisual ministries
  Composition
  Design
  Production
  Distribution

Writing ministries
  Free-lance
  Curriculum development
  Fiction
  Non-fiction
  Editing
  Institutional communications
  Journalistic skills for publications

Teaching ministries
  Sunday school: children, youth,
    students, women
  Grade school
  High school
  College

Music ministries
  Composition
  Training

Ministries to youth
  Teaching
  Sponsoring
  Open houses and recreation
  Outings and trips
  Counseling
  Academic assistance

Sports ministries
  Neighborhood teams
  Church teams

Therapeutic counseling
  Independent
  Church-based
  Institutional

Radio and television ministries
  Technical assistance
  Writing
  Announcing
  Producing

Theater and drama ministries
  Acting
  Directing
  Writing
  Scheduling

Social ministries
  Literacy
  Pro-life
  Pro-decency
  Housing
  Safety
  Beautification
  Drug rehabilitation

Performance
  Voice
  Choir
  Instrumentalist

Evangelistic ministries
  Personal witnessing
  Parachurch groups
  Home Bible studies
  Outreach to children
  Visitation teams
  Counseling at meetings
  Telephone counseling

Pastoral care assistance
  Visitation
  Newcomer welcoming and assistance
  Hospitality
  Food and clothing and transportation

Prayer ministries
  Praying
  Mobilizing for prayer events
  Helping with small groups of prayer
  Coordinating prayer chains
  Promoting prayer days and weeks
    and vigils

Missions
  All of the above across cultures

Support ministries
  Countless "secular" jobs that
    undergird other ministries

The awesome significance of
  motherhood

Making a home as a full-time wife

I realize this list is incomplete and reflects my own culture and limitations. But it is worth the risk, I think, to make clear that the vision of manhood and womanhood presented in this book is not meant to hinder ministry but to purify and empower it in a pattern of Biblical obedience.

The ninth affirmation of the Danvers Statement[32] is perhaps the crucial final thing to say so that the aim of this book is not misunderstood.

> With half the world's population outside the reach of indigenous evangelism; with countless other lost people in those societies that have heard the gospel; with the stresses and miseries of sickness, malnutrition, homelessness, illiteracy, ignorance, aging, addiction, crime, incarceration, neuroses, and loneliness, no man or woman who feels a passion from God to make His grace known in word and deed need ever live without a fulfilling ministry for the glory of Christ and the good of this fallen world.

Notes

1. Between November, 1983 and May, 1984 I carried on a debate concerning this issue with my friends and former colleagues Alvera and Berkeley Mickelsen in our denominational periodical, *The Standard* (of the Baptist General Conference). In these monthly articles I tried to lay the exegetical foundations for how men and women are called by God to relate to each other. The names of the articles are: "Male, Female and Morality" (November, 1983), pp. 26-28; "Satan's Design in Reversing Male Leadership Role" (December, 1983), pp. 33-35; "Jesus' Teaching on Men and Women: Dismantling the Fall, Not the Creation" (January, 1984), pp. 32-34; "A Metaphor of Christ and the Church" (February, 1984), pp. 27-29; "Creation, Culture and Corinthian Prophetesses" (March, 1984), pp. 30-32; "The Order of Creation" (April, 1984), pp. 35-38; "How Should a Woman Lead?" (May, 1984), pp. 34-36.

2. The cassette tapes of seven sermons on manhood and womanhood can be ordered by writing to Council of Biblical Manhood and Womanhood, P.O. Box 1173, Wheaton, IL 60189.

3. Paul K. Jewett, *Man as Male and Female* (Grand Rapids: William B. Eerdmans Pub. Co., 1975), p. 172.

4. *Man as Male and Female*, p. 173. The reference is to Emil Brunner, *Das Gebot und die Ordnungen* (Tuebingen: J.C.B. Mohr, 1933), p. 358.

5. *Man as Male and Female*, p. 178.

6. *Man as Male and Female,* p. 187f.

7. The teaching in 1 Peter 3:1-7 concerning the differentiation of roles is not based explicitly on the order of creation, but neither is it based on convention. Rather it is rooted in the example of "holy women who hoped in God" (v. 5). Sarah is cited as an example of submission, not because she complied with Abraham's wish that she pose as his sister (Genesis 20), which is the amazing example of submission we might have expected Peter to use, but rather because she said "my lord" when speaking offhandedly to herself about her husband. This seems to suggest that the root of Sarah's submission was a deep allegiance to Abraham's leadership that expressed itself without coercion or public pressure.

8. This is developed and defended exegetically in two extensive essays by John Sailhammer and Ray Ortlund Jr. in *Recovering Biblical Manhood and Womanhood* (Crossway Books, 1990).

9. The limitation of this essay is seen, for example, in that I will say very little about the capacity of a woman to bear children, and the special role that she has in nursing and nurturing them. Nor do I say anything about the man's crucial role in nurturing healthy, secure children. My focus is on the significance that manhood and womanhood have for the relational dynamics between men and women and the implications of these dynamics for the roles appropriate for each.

10. The fact that a Christian wife and church member, according to Acts 2:17, may "prophesy" implies, at least, that she may often have ideas and insights that a wise and humble husband and pastor will listen to and adopt. On women and prophecy see Wayne Grudem, *The Gift of Prophecy: In the New Testament and Today* (Wheston: Crossway Books, 1988), pp. 215-225.

11. This understanding of masculine responsibility will be developed, for example, from the way God comes to Adam first after the fall, implying his special responsibility in the failure even though Eve had sinned first. This accords with other pointers in the early chapters of Genesis before the fall that God meant for Adam to have a special responsibility for leadership (establishing a pattern of initiative) in relation to Eve. The sharing of initiatives within that general pattern is implied in the image of Christ and the church as the model for mar-

riage (Ephesians 5:21-33). Christ means for his bride to look to him for leadership, but not to the exclusion of her own thoughtful choices and initiatives in communication and in shared mission.

12. James Dobson, *Straight Talk to Men and Their Wives* (Waco: Word Books, 1980), pp. 64f.

13. Notice the move from "Children, obey your *parents*" in Ephesians 6:1 to "*Fathers* . . . bring them up in the nurture and discipline of the Lord" (v. 4). Both have responsibility to discipline, and children should hold both in high regard. But there is a special responsibility on fathers for the moral life and discipline of the home.

14. The Biblical teaching on nature's voice urging men and women not to exchange or confuse the cultural symbols of masculinity and femininity is very relevant here. When Paul says in 1 Corinthians 11:14, "Does not *nature teach* you that for a man to wear long hair is degrading to him?" he means that there is in man a *native sense* of repugnance against taking on cultural symbols of femininity. We would say, "Does not nature teach you that it is degrading to a man to wear a dress to church?" This voice of "nature" has great social benefits even in cultures untouched by special revelation from Scripture. But Romans 1:18-32 shows that a culture can become so corrupted that the native sense is ignored (vv. 26-27) and suppressed so that unnatural practices are even approved (v. 32). At such a point the call for Biblical repentance is not only a call to believe what the Bible teaches, but also to be transformed so deeply that the natural inclinations of mature manhood and womanhood are recovered, and society conforms once again not merely to what the Scriptures teach, but to "what nature teaches" among those who are now under the sway of Biblical truth and, more widely, under the rectifying social power of common grace. Alongside this teaching on the voice of nature should be put the teaching of 1 Corinthians 13:5 that love does not act in an "unseemly" way; it does not offend against good manners.

15. Another pointer from Scripture that this is the way God intends the relationship of husband and wife to be is the image of Christ as head of the church with man playing that role toward his wife according to Ephesians 5:23. The image of head implies that Christ is the *provider* as well as a leader. "Hold fast to the *Head, from whom the whole body,*

nourished and knit together through its joints and ligaments, grows with a growth that is from God" (Colossians 2:19; cf. Ephesians 4:16).

This does not at all contradict the idea of leadership implied in "headship." On the contrary it strengthens it. The thought in Colossians 2:19 begins in verse 18 with a reference to people who are puffed up, "not holding fast to the Head, from whom the whole body, nourished and knit together through its joints and ligaments, grows with a growth that is from God." What is especially significant here for us is the implication that since Christ as head is *supplier,* the church must "hold fast" to him. The opposite of holding fast is being puffed up in mind and independent of Christ. So the implication is that headship is a role to be depended on and followed. There is to be an allegiance to the head as provider. This in essence implies a kind of leadership role for the head, as one to whom the body should ever look for what it needs. This is all the more evident when we note how Christ in fact does provide for his wife, the church. As the head he provides the body with truth (Ephesians 4:15, 21) and strength (Colossians 1:11) and wisdom (Colossians 2:3) and love (Ephesians 3:17-18; 4:16; Colossians 2:2). This means that the idea of provider implies loving leader because Christ leads with his truth and wisdom and he does this with love that lives out his teaching before us and for us.

There are numerous other Biblical evidences of the father's special responsibility to provide for his family. Consider, for example, 1 Timothy 3:5, "For if someone (an elder) does not know how to manage *(proistenai)* his own household, how shall he take care of *(epimelesetai)* the church of God?" This idea of managing his own home well may have more than provision in mind (leadership for sure; see the use of *proistemi* in 1 Thessalonians 5:12), but I doubt that it has less. Elders/overseers are responsible to feed (1 Peter 5:2; Acts 20:28; Jeremiah 3:15) and protect (Acts 20:28-31) the flock.

Other evidences of the father's special responsibility to provide for his family portray the husband and father as the protector too. For example, Deuteronomy 10:18, "[God] executes justice for the fatherless and the widow, and loves the stranger giving him food and raiment." In other words, when the natural protector and provider is not

there God steps in to take his place for the orphan and widow.
Jeremiah 31:32 points in this same direction. God says concerning
Israel, "My covenant which they broke, though I was their husband,
says the Lord." How was he their husband? The context suggests that
he was their husband in giving them protection at the sea and the provision in the wilderness.

16. The Biblical support for this is seen first in the texts like the ones cited
above in note 10 (Deuteronomy 10:18 and Jeremiah 31:32). It is also
implied in Ephesians 5:25, "Husbands, love your wives as Christ
loved the church and gave himself up for her." Christ is here
sacrificing himself to protect his wife, the church, from the ravages of
sin and hell. Christ gives himself as the model for the husband in this
regard because the husband is the *man*. This is not an arbitrary assign-
ment. It is fitting because men were *created* for this. The "mystery" of
marriage (Ephesians 5:32) is the truth that God designed male and
female from the beginning to carry different responsibilities on the
analogy of Christ and his church. The sense of responsibility to protect is there in man by virtue of this design of creation, not by virtue
of the marriage covenant. Marriage makes the burden more personal
and more intense, but it does not create it.

Additional support for man's primary responsibility to protect
women is found in the Old Testament pattern of men, rather than
women, being given the duty to go to war. And nature itself seems to
teach this duty of protection by endowing men, by and large, with
greater brute strength.

17. Such customs, like all manners, are easily caricatured and satirized.
But that is a mark of immaturity. Just as men and women know that
some rough contact sports are not natural for women to play, so we
know that there is a verbal rough-and-tumble among men, a kind of
tough and rugged argumentation that is less appropriate when speaking to a woman than to a man.

18. J. I. Packer, "Understanding the Differences," in *Women, Authority and
the Bible*, ed. by Alvera Mickelsen (Downers Grove: InterVarsity Press,
1986), p. 298-299.

19. One way of relating this definition to Scripture is to see it as an
attempt to unfold some of what is implied in the old-fashioned phrase

"help meet" in Genesis 2:18—"And the Lord God said, It is not good that the man should be alone; I will make him a help meet for him" (KJV). It may well be that the feminine inclination to help a man in his life and work signifies far more than I have been able to spell out in the phrases "affirm, receive, and nurture." But I have chosen to focus on what seems to me to be the heart of woman's feminine suitableness to man as a helper. The animals were helpful in some ways (Genesis 2:19). But the helpfulness of the woman is radically different. That unique human element is what I am interested in.

20. Ronda Chervin, *Feminine, Free and Faithful* (San Francisco: Ignatius Press, 1986), p. 15.

21. The Biblical warrant for this definition is 1 Peter 3:1-6, where a believing wife is married to an unbelieving husband. The text clearly teaches that she is to be submissive, but not in such a way that follows him in his unbelief. In fact, she is instructed how to get him to change, and be converted. The implication here is that her submission is not a de facto yielding to all that he says (since she has a higher allegiance to Jesus), but a *disposition* to yield and an *inclination* to follow. Her submission is a readiness to support his leadership wherever it does not lead to sin.

22. This paragraph is taken largely from my wider discussion of this issue in *Desiring God* (Portland: Multnomah Press, 1986), pp. 177-184.

23. For example, Gerald Sheppard, a professor of Old Testament at the University of Toronto, said in 1986, "I believe that the Gospel—as Evangelicals Concerned recognizes—should lead us at least to an affirmation of gay and lesbian partnerships ruled by a biblical ethic analogous to that offered for heterosexual relationships." "A Response to Anderson (II)," *TSF Bulletin*, Vol. 9, No. 4, (March-April, 1986), p. 21. Similarly in July of 1986 the Evangelical Women's Caucus International under the influence of Virginia Mollenkott and Nancy Hardesty took a stand affirming the legitimacy of lesbianism to such an extent that members like Katherine Kroeger and Gretchen Hull withdrew their membership. See "Gay Rights Resolution Divides Membership of Evangelical Women's Caucus," in: *Christianity Today* (October 3, 1986), pp. 40-44. Ralph Blair, the founder of Evangelicals Concerned, continues to debunk the claim that homosexuals can or

should change their sexual orientation. He promotes monogamous homosexual relationships and claims Biblical support for it, arguing that the Bible is opposed to promiscuous homosexuality, not homosexuality itself. His views are cited by Tim Stafford, "Coming Out," *Christianity Today* (August 18, 1989), p. 19.

24. For a discussion of contemporary ministries that believe in the real possibilities of homosexuals to experience significant changes in the focus and power of their sexual preference see *Christianity Today*, August 18, 1989. See also George Rekers, *Shaping Your Child's Sexual Identity* (Grand Rapids: Baker Book House, 1982).

25. This is implied in the goodness and gladness of creation before the fall (Genesis 2) when man, created first, was called to the primary responsibility of leadership, and woman, created to be "a helper suitable for him," was called to use her gifts in helping carry that leadership through. This was all "very good" (Genesis 1:31) and therefore must have given man and woman great gladness. The same glad responsiveness to this order of things is implied in Ephesians 5:21-33 where man and wife are to model their relationship after that of Christ and the church. The church delights to accept strength and leadership from Christ. The delight that a woman takes in the strength and leadership of her husband is not merely owing to the marriage covenant. Just as man was created with a native sense of responsibility to lead and provide and protect in ways appropriate to his varying relationships (see note 12), so woman was created as a suitable complement to honor this responsibility with gladness and satisfaction.

26. See page 50 for some examples of feminine strengths that enrich men.

27. Weldon M. Hardenbrook, *Missing from Action: Vanishing Manhood in America* (Nashville: Thomas Nelson Publishers, 1987), pp. 9-10.

28. Experience and psychology teach us that there are significant differences of many kinds between men and women. In each case one could establish a standard that would make one sex stronger and the other weaker. But Paul's teaching on the body of Christ warns us against demeaning those that have traits of weakness—male or female (1 Corinthians 12:21-26). The creation of male and female in the image of God (Genesis 1:27) forbids that we make our diversity a ground for variable worth as persons in God's eyes. And the Biblical

declaration that all was "very good" when God created us with our differences means that a "weakness" by one narrow standard is a "strength" in its contribution to the total fabric of man as male and female in God's image.

29. When 1 Peter 3:7 refers to the wife as a "weaker feminine vessel," it is probably focussing on the most obvious fact, especially in that more rugged culture, that a woman has lesser brute strength. That is, she is more in need of protection and provision from the man than he is from her. He is to "recognize" this and honor her by supplying all she needs as a fellow-heir of grace. The verse does not contemplate the question I have raised, namely whether there are some other things about man that can also be described as weaker than woman.

30. I am assuming implicitly here what I said about submission on pp. 51-52.

31. The elders are charged with the primary responsibility of leadership (Acts 20:28; 1 Timothy 5:17; 1 Peter 5:3) and Biblical instruction (Titus 1:9; 1 Timothy 3:2; 5:17) in the church. That's a summary of their job. So when Paul puts those two things together and says, "I do not permit a woman to teach or exercise authority," one very natural implication is, "I do not permit a woman to assume the office of elder in the church."

So the authority Paul has in mind in 1 Timothy 2:12 at least includes the authority of elders. We saw already from Jesus in Luke 22:26 what that is supposed to look like: "Let the greatest among you become as the youngest, and the leader as one who serves." Paul said in 2 Corinthians 10:8 and 13:10 that God gave him authority in the church not for tearing down or destroying, but for building up. And Peter said to the elders of the churches (1 Peter 5:3), "Do not domineer over the those in your charge, but be examples to the flock."

In other words elder-authority is servant-authority. Elder-leadership is servant-leadership. That's why teaching is at the heart of this calling. Biblical authority leads by persuasion—by teaching—not by coercion or political maneuvering. Elder-authority is always subordinate to Biblical truth. Therefore teaching is the primary instrument of leadership in the church. And authority refers to the divine calling of spiritual, gifted men to take primary responsibility as elders for

Christlike, servant-leadership and teaching in the church. Their goal is not their own status or honor. Their goal is the equipping of the saints—women and men—to do the work of the ministry.

32. The Danvers Statement is the charter statement (Rationale, Purposes and Affirmations) of the Council on Biblical Manhood and Womanhood and may be ordered from the Council at P.O. Box 1173, Wheaton, IL 60189.

⚜ desiringGod

If you would like to further explore the vision of God and life presented in this book, we at Desiring God would love to serve you. We have hundreds of resources to help you grow in your passion for Jesus Christ and help you spread that passion to others. At our website, desiringGod.org, you'll find almost everything John Piper has written and preached, including more than thirty books. We've made over twenty-five years of his sermons available free online for you to read, listen to, download, and in some cases watch.

In addition, you can access hundreds of articles, listen to our daily internet radio program, find out where John Piper is speaking, learn about our conferences, discover our God-centered children's curricula, and browse our online store. John Piper receives no royalties from the books he writes and no compensation from Desiring God. The funds are all reinvested into our gospel-spreading efforts. DG also has a whatever-you-can-afford policy, designed for individuals with limited discretionary funds. If you'd like more information about this policy, please contact us at the address or phone number below. We exist to help you treasure Jesus Christ and his gospel above all things because he is most glorified in you when you are most satisfied in him. Let us know how we can serve you!

Desiring God
Post Office Box 2901
Minneapolis, Minnesota 55402

888.346.4700
mail@desiringGod.org
www.desiringGod.org

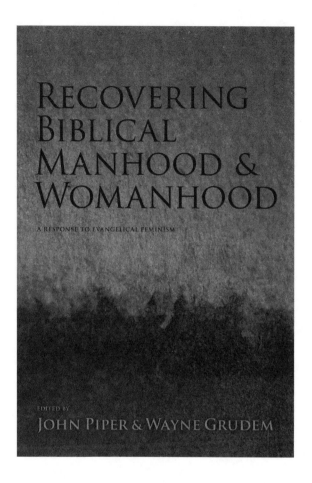

RECOVERING
BIBLICAL
MANHOOD &
WOMANHOOD

A RESPONSE TO EVANGELICAL FEMINISM

EDITED BY
JOHN PIPER & WAYNE GRUDEM

Feminist ideology is everywhere. It's in schools, television shows, music, politics—even the church. In fact, it's so pervasive within the evangelical community that it's become its own movement—"evangelical feminism." But what many of its adherents fail to recognize is that incorporating feminism into theology has devastating implications on our relationships, society, the church, and our homes.

In the most comprehensive response yet, a group of scholars explore every key passage of Scripture to determine the biblical view of male and female roles and relationships. What they have found is imperative for anyone searching for the truth.